# INTRODUCTION

HERE IT IS–the publishing scoop of the century!! Nessie has at last broken her silence to write her very own autobiography.

From the depths of Loch Ness we bring you the amusing and entertaining story of a happy lady who always has the last laugh.

Published by Lang Syne Publishers Ltd
45 Finnieston St., Glasgow
Tel: 041-204 3104
Printed by Dave Barr Print
45 Finnieston Street, Glasgow
Tel: 041-221 2598

Reprinted 1992

*Some people actually question my existance!*

# CHAPTER ONE

WITH ALL THESE scientists and camera experts about nowadays, breathing down my neck as you might say (and there's plenty of room for them, for my neck is nearly fifteen feet long) I think it is time I told my side of the story. Straight from the monster's mouth.

To be honest I have always considered the descriptions of me to be most unfair. A monster conjures up the picture of a fearsome beast of violent temper, whereas I am the gentlest of creatures; placid I am, and personally, so far as looks are concerned, I consider myself beautiful, proving that there are exceptions to the present fashionable saying: "small is beautiful". "LARGE" is sure beautiful in my case for, as well as a fifteen feet long neck, my body adds another fifteen feet. And then there's my tail.

Now, before going any further, I think I should clear up the question of my species. I know I am called "Nessie" after the loch of my home but officially I should be called "Plesiosaurus".

The dictionary says a plesiosaurus is—"an extinct" (ha, ha) "marine reptile of the Mesozoic Period in Europe and in North America, with a long neck, small head and all four limbs developed as paddles."

That's me near enough—except that my "paddles" have evolved to hands and feet; and I am partial to a frilly finny edge or two as decoration—a vanity I believe, frowned upon in the scientific world as a frivolity not expected from the likes of me.

Ah well, one has to try and improve one's image beyond this plesiosaurus label.

*Humps appeared around their boat.*

Another work of learning remarks: "The plesiosaurus is one of the earliest forms of life amongst the great water dwelling reptiles, now long extinct" (Ha, ha!). "It was certainly a strange monster for, to the head of a lizard were united the teeth of a crocodile, a long neck like that of a serpent, the ribs of a chameleon and the paddles of a whale."

I have been hearing with astonishment that some human beings actually question my existence. Cynics say that I am a publicity stunt invented by, and existing only in the imagination of the Scottish Tourist Board.

These cynics think they clinch their case by pointing out that I am only reported as appearing in the holiday season. Never fear, I'm around all the time—it's just that when I surface in the winter, there are no holidaymakers to see me.

Down through the years there have been so many sightings of me—apart from the mistaken ones, when a floating log or extra large wave is spotted as me— that surely no one in his or her senses can now doubt that I am HERE!

I mean how else can one account for the two Inverness men out boating being suddenly surrounded by humps, like, as they said afterwards—as if they had been in the middle of a school of whales; and that awesome moment when each hump went off in a different direction! (You will understand how this is possible when I come to discuss the family). Nor should one ever forget the man who gave up his job, and all honour to him, to settle by Loch Ness to watch...and watch...and watch...

I began to be seen, or more correctly, *noticed*, in the 1930's. Since then more and more folk from all over the world have attempted to make my aquaintance. They include a zoologist from the Royal Ontario Museum in Toronto, a professor from the Massachusetts Institute of Technology, a band of scientists from the Academy of Applied Sciences of New York and film makers from Japan—to name but a few.

Yet there is no need to go any further than a place of residence by the shores of Loch Ness for a convincing example of a man who saw me plain. And he was a *holy* man, too, not given to "terminological inexactitudes" (a phrase coined by Winston Churchill in the House of Commons when wishing not to offend by the simple word "lie"). Yes, this holy man was a monk of the Abbey of Fort Augustus at the end of the Loch. (One *knows* a benedictine is a liqueur of potent quality, but it does *not* induce hallucination).

And while we are on the subject of holy men, it may astonish you to learn that the monk of Fort Augustus was not the first holy man to see me—at least, not me, but my great, great, truly great, grandmother. That was in the year 565 A.D.! He was of course Saint Columba.

*Aha! The Japanese film men are here . . .*

St Columba had come across from Ireland, where the first Scots hailed from, to visit the Pictish chiefs and try and convert them to Christianity. This worthy mission included a visit to a minor king of the Picts called Brude whose fort was stationed where Inverness now stands.

It was during a contemplative solitary walk by the shores of Loch Ness that the saint saw my five times removed grandmother. On return to Brude's encampment he told me of what he had seen.

In the words of his biographer St. Adamnan: "The monster did rush up with a great roar and open mouth but when the saint commanded it to retreat, it obeyed".

I can understand that being so, for 1 remember some of my elderly relatives were, unlike me, of an irascible nature, yet, on being defied, would display the cowardly streak in their nature.

Thus you will realise that we of Loch Ness, us so called monsters, have been around for quite a long time. As further witness of this, the scientists exploring here, have discovered stone circles of apparent prehistoric origin on the bed of the Loch at about 50 feet below the surface. They thus argue that at one time the Loch must have been at least 50 feet lower than now. But of course! It was my ancestors' arrival in the Loch—their concerted bulk, which caused the waters to rise!

I come into the story of Loch Ness on November 1, 1755. On that day I was born deep in these waters. And they were in a proper state that day—not because of my arrival, but because of an earthquake centred on Lisbon. Yes, an earthquake so far off as present day Portugal, stirred us up in Loch Ness.

I quote: "Loch Ness, on account of its great depth, never freezes... there is a geological fault along the line of the Great Glen of which Loch Ness occupies about half of the length—a line of permanent weakness in the Earth's crust. "This accounts for the happening on November 1st 1755 when, during a great earthquake centred on Lisbon, the waters of Loch Ness became violently agitated; and a series of waves rolled along the Loch to the upper end and, dashing for some 200 yards up the course of the River Oich which rose five feet above its usual level... This phenonomenon lasting for about an hour before the surface of the river and the Loch resumed their wonted calm."

If faraway Lisbon could disturb our Loch, then it proves that we are deep. Very deep.

*I'm born — and it was quite a day!*

In the 19th century there was a Captain Orton who was rowed out to the middle of the Loch where he began to unwind a weighted plumb line. Down and down went that plumb line until a whole giant barrel of it had disappeared into the depths...and still it had not reached the bed of the Loch.

This explains the difficulties of those who would hunt me with their sophisticated equipment—the tremendous depth of the Loch which could be said to almost cut Scotland in half.

And I have my own theory on how this near cutting in half, was extended south of Loch Ness. I think my ancestors unwittingly helped the formation of the Great Glen comprising Loch Ness, Loch Oich and Loch Lochy.

Let us suppose that a group of these aforesaid relatives of mine, huge even in comparison with me, got tired of being pestered by the P.T.B. (Pictish Tourist Board) and in a desperate attempt to win peace and privacy, left Loch Ness in a floundering mass to head south-west where instinct told them there was the wide sea.

Their passage scored the land deeply. They made the indentations for the beds of Loch Oich and indeed of Loch Lochy...but at that point, exhaustion overtook the would be travellers and a home sickness came upon them and they returned—this double journey laying the basis of the line of the Caledonian Canal which today links the North Sea with the Atlantic Ocean.

But to return to the present day. My husband (you're surprised?)—my husband and I have a family, somewhat grown expansively in these passing years; but in the dark depths of these waters it is a problem keeping tabs on them and indeed if questioned on with how many we have been blessed, I'm afraid it would be but guesswork.

Much as I favour sporting around on occasion near the surface, the same cannot be said for the rest of us who are shy of human beings; but it is always possible on a sighting, that the sightseer is not seeing me at all but either my husband or one of my children on one of their rare ventures to the surface.

You should know that I am very sorry for the scientists, when I think of the trouble and expense they have undergone to record my presence and so far with comparatively little success.

My Scottish nature—Scottish, through auld aquaintance with the land—shudders at the thought of the expense. Think of the cost alone of taking from 50,000 to 100,000 separate photographs! Think of exposing in one instance 46,000 negatives two of which showed a salmon and one other...an eel.

*My great great great grandmother was ordered to retreat by Saint Columba
— and she did!*

One must admire the persistence of such men, and of the elaborateness of the preparations—of having a control room in a cottage by the Loch with a television screen manned to watch the under water place where cameras both cinematic and still are set up to "shoot" me. ·

The operator at the television screen can press a button should I appear, which would bring yet more recording apparatus into motion—for already, one camera set automatically had been taking a picture by an extra powerful under water flash every fifteen seconds!

All of that brings me to the crux of the matter and its an important fact that scientists and professors have seemingly overlooked. I instinctively shy away from bright light!

On top of all that I now find that bookmakers have opened a book on me: they are offering odds of 33 to 1 against my being in existence!

Shops are even selling plastic models of my goodself and meat pastries which, I'm told, are delicious. Needless to say I can't claim a penny in royalties!

Really, it gets more and more difficult to get away from it all and savour the kind of peaceful existence that prevailed in my great great etc grandmother's day. If only Saint Columba had kept quiet about seeing her, I might never have been bothered today.

Talking of keeping quiet: if things get any more disturbing then I am considering swimming down the River Ness some dark night and striking out to sea and to a new life

Ah...but it would be sad to leave the old place after all these years. And it would be a kindness for me to try to help the scientists after all their trouble—

But I DO NOT like bright light. That is why possibly the nearest to a satisfactory recording of my presence was not by sight but, *by sound*. That happened a year or so ago when a marine biologist from Australia was asked by the World Life Research Institute—a United States Government sponsored body based in California, to go to Loch Ness with his sound equipment.

Thus, on a day of the Scottish Highlands' brief but beautiful summer, he lowered from an inflatable boat on Loch Ness, under water loud speakers which sent down tape-recorded signals while at the same time his sonar apparatus scanned the depths. His loudspeaker signals were responded to by a large mobile shape ascending from great depth up to between 200 and 250 feet under the surface, at which depth it came into the range of the sonar beams resulting in a clear sonar "picture" or graph, recording a solid moving

*Captain Orton tried a plumb line to establish the depth of the loch.*

object between 30 to 50 feet long and of near 7 feet deep in bulk.

Me? I leave the reader to judge if that was not the most convincing result of any of the "hunts" to date.

Mind, my lifestyle has its funny side ("funny ha, ha" as well as "funny peculiar"). Consider the young Englishman, sponsored, not by the U.S. Government but by the British Bacon Curers Federation who came to the Loch with a hot air balloon as the principal item in their equipment.

The idea was that they should ascend some distance above the surface of the Loch and lower a rope, on the end of which hung *a large chunk of ham.*

The balloon would then move along above the surface of the Loch with the ham trailing enticingly as bait, a foot or two above the waters. They then hoped that I would leap like a salmon and break surface to get the ham in my jaws. And hang on? Really!

What did happen was very simple. Nature took a hand and chose when the balloon rose from the land, to send a contrary wind about the place, blowing the balloon, not across the water but careering above an adjoining field where it crashed after a flight of half a mile or so—in the wrong direction. Some say that afterwards great bubbles appeared on the surface of the Loch.


Submarine laughter?

And finally, the advertisement which appeared a year or two ago in the New York Times with the heading: "Have a picnic with the Loch Ness monster", proposing an adventurous journey by jet for 100 tourists from the States to Scotland; and a sojourn by the waterside of Loch Ness. By Drumnadrochit's Glenurquhart Bay for example—reputed to be one of my visiting places?


One thing I'll say in conclusion. If any of you folks come to Loch Ness and capture a really clear detailed photograph of me, then undoubtedly your fortune will be made!

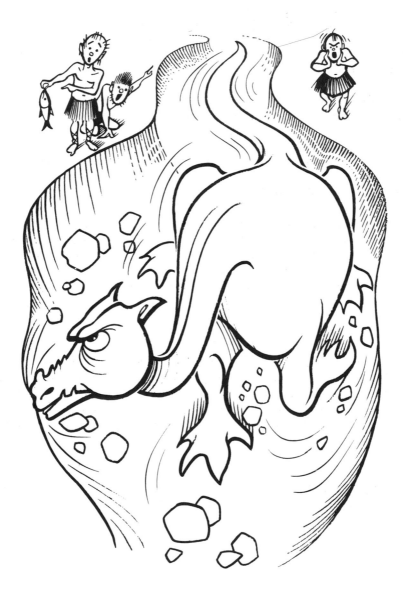

*An ancestor fed-up with the Pictish Tourist Board?*

# CHAPTER TWO

WHEN I feel like cheering myself up I have a read through my diary. Over the centuries I have derived great pleasure from recording all the daft things folk have tried to bring me out into the open.

So if I'm feeling a bit fed up I go through my memoirs—to date there are 327 volumes to choose from—and have a jolly good laugh.

I always like recalling the occasion when I had allegedly been captured after going on a man-eating spree! As I'm a vegetarian that one was a bit hard to swallow at first but my husband soon had me seeing the funny side.

The German paper which carried the story fooled many of their readers with its report that I had been taken to Glasgow in a huge cage. The only clue as to the real truth of the story lay in the date at the top of every page. Yes it was April 1—All Fools Day.

Some other recent highlights include—

January, 1976: Attractive girl divers came all the way from Nottingham in the hope that their beauty might lure me to the surface. I was too busy doing chores but my sons had a super time!

That same month it was reassuring to learn from Parliament that the Government have powers to protect me through the Secretary of State for Scotland should the worst ever come to the worst. It was kind of two English M.P.s to take time from other duties to inquire about my wellbeing.

*I've got quite a handful of youngsters to bring up . . .*

FORT AUGUSTUS—I SOMETIMES TAKE A STROLL HERE WHEN THE VILLAGERS ARE ASLEEP

CASTLE URQUHART ON THE SHORES OF THE LOCH—MY HOME IS VERY NEAR HERE

ABOVE AND BELOW: THE LOCH THE WAY I LIKE IT—NOT A PERSON IN SIGHT!

AS ITHERS SEE ME—MY MODEL ON THE LOCH! FRANK GRAY, THE FAMOUS PHOTOGRAPHER WHO TOOK THIS WOULD LOVE ONE OF ME BUT...

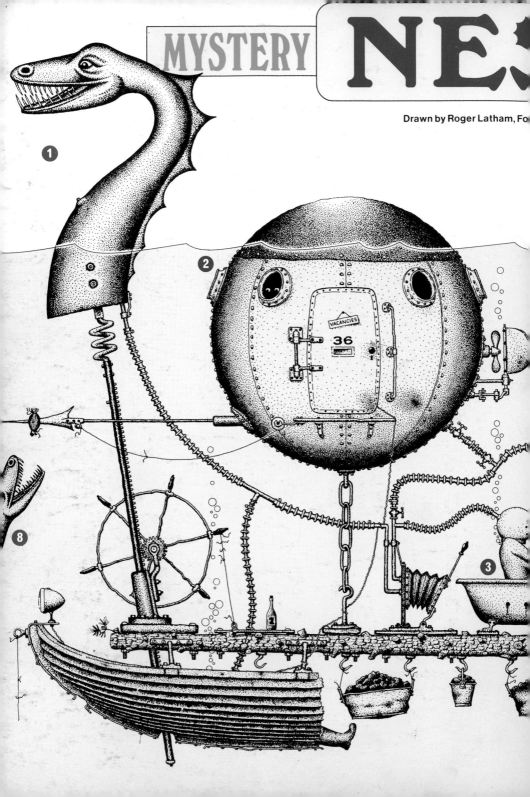

Drawn by Roger Latham, Fo

# SSIE

# SOLVED!

...ness IV1 2XY. Copyright ©1988

## 'Taking the myth out of Nessie'

1. Nessie classic pose. Flexible mounting makes it impossible to get a sharp photograph.
2. Detachable fore-hump and living quarters, self-propelled for single hump displays.
3. Bonny wee Morag MacAbre, intrepid oarswoman and owner of The Loch Ness Monster.
4. Aft-hump with computer-designed flipper-brake to create mysterious surface swirls.
5. The 'Swivelling Jock' mechanism for generating inexplicable standing waves.
6. Jet thrust unit to propel Nessie round her busy schedule of summer appearances.
7. Entrance to the Loch Ness—Loch Morar link tunnel...yes, it really does exist!

LOCH MORAR
47 MILES

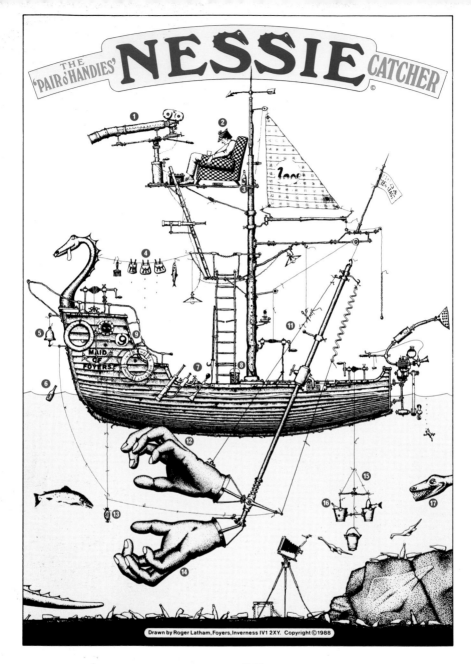

# THE 'PAIR ò HANDIES' NESSIE CATCHER ©

Drawn by Roger Latham, Foyers, Inverness IV1 2XY. Copyright © 1988

1. Movie camera, to film Nessie in close-up, pin-sharp, living detail...
2. Wee Angus McOatup, the ever-vigilant monster spotter.
3. Lunch.
4. Alternative bait: neep 'n' onion and tattie cocktail flavours.
5. Monster alarm system.
6. Breakfast.
7. Side-scan sonar facility with long range optical back-up.
8. Paint for spotting monsters.
9. Nine.
10. A genuine photograph of Nessie the Loch Ness Monster.
11. Monster catching operations nerve-centre.
12. Upper hand.
13. An adult black-face haggis, steeped in whisky—Nessie's favourite!
14. Underhand.
15. Multi-bucket dredge, to collect sediment samples (and chill supper)
16. Supper.

THEY'LL NEVER CAPTURE ME ON FILM!

EVENING—MY FAVOURITE TIME OF DAY

I'M DOWN THERE SOMEWHERE

THE RIVER NESS AT INVERNESS—I NEVER GO UP TO THE BIG TOWN. IT'S TOO NOISY!

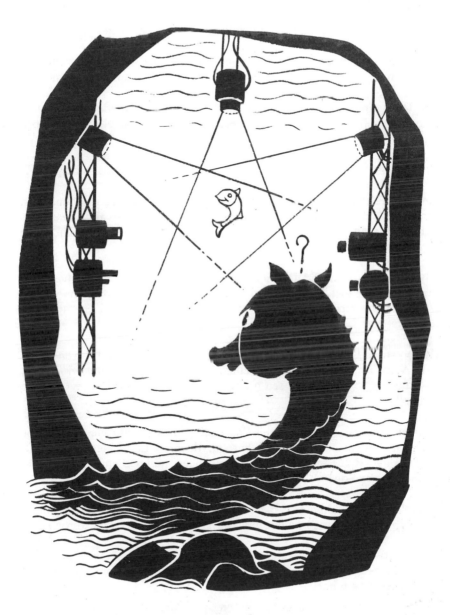

*I didn't fall for the bright lights trap!*

During January it was also claimed that giant underwater caverns and tunnels run from Loch Ness which might mean that I travel between the loch and the Moray Firth.

Where do I go on my holidays? I'm not saying!

A few days later I found myself being described as a sunken Viking ship.

April: News is announced of a new monster hunt and it even makes front page news in many of America's leading newspapers. How's that for fame!

And folk going on a cruise up the Loch can now get themselves insured against a bite from me. Adults are covered for up to £2,000; children for up to £500.

Controversy still rages over a recently released portrait said to be of me.

June: Scientist chappies talk about salmon being a great favourite of mine and they hope that a glimpse of me might be caught at Urquhart Bay. Feeling is that I lay in wait there to pounce on the shoals of salmon waiting to run up the River Enrick.

July: I'm to be a film star! The Japs are set to make a movie on my adventures after I leave the loch to go on a world tour. And the T.V. people announce a new adventure series about me but it's to be filmed on Loch Lomond. I feel like a Rangers fan sentenced to watch Celtic for six months!

My good friends from across the Atlantic get an unusual offer from an advert in the *New York Times*. "Have a picnic with the Loch Ness Monster" it said. And the cost of coming to see me was £350 per person. Hope they like salmon!!

October: Goodness me what's this I'm reading in the papers: Nessie could be facing an unexpected hazard in her lair deep in Loch Ness—RADIO-ACTIVITY. Radioactive isotopes have been pumped into the loch to measure water flow.

The folk in officialdom said there is absolutely no danger and nothing to worry about. I'm reassured but will still keep a few dozen toes crossed.

November: British punters stand to gain £280,000 if I show myself after taking advantage of odds offered by a big firm of bookmakers. Naturally I would like to help but...

December: I know you human folk enjoy a cuppa but this is ridiculous: Reports the Daily Telegraph: "Expedition expert says that the loch is full of teapots. There seem to be more teapots than anything else."

February, 1977. A newspaper reports that an American plans to lay several large lobster-pot style traps in a bid to capture me. Each would be baited with fish and will contain an electric trigger system which will close the trap and warn humans on the surface at the same time.

April: News that a submarine is coming to look for me. Is it yellow?

July, 1978: Underwater loudspeakers are to be used as part of a plan to attract me. Where did I put those earplugs?

Those Jap film chaps are still busy and a replica is at present under construction in that far and distant land. Will it look like me?

A punter has placed an accumulator worth £5 million. He has £1 on a dry weekend, Nessie, creatures from outer space and a 100—1 long shot called Ragabash in the 2.30 at Newbury.

Weather note: It's raining so I shan't go out today.

Hot news from America: The fabled Loch Ness Monster certainly exists and the loch is probably home to a colony of up to 30 of the creatures, the like of which mankind may never have known, a U.S. expert said in Boston, Massachusetts.

My goodness, look at the time. Where are those children. It's way past their bedtime!

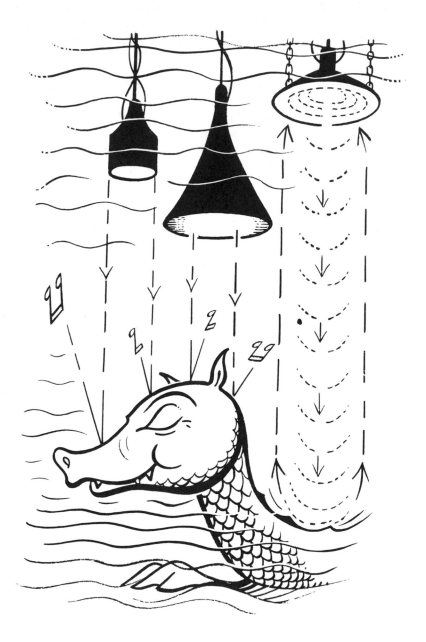

*They tried to lure me up with the sound of underwater loudspeakers — but it didn't work!*

# CHAPTER THREE

THE THOUSANDS of people who **don't** believe that I exist are probably doing me a good turn.

Their firm views, repeated in shops, offices, factories and hostelries all over the land, help throw up a useful smokescreen which does nothing but good for our family privacy here in the loch.

They probably won't even believe a word of this very autobiography. I can almost hear them saying: "It's all made up!" and "Nessie... writing a book! Nonsense!"

Of course so many daft stories exist about Scotland and things Scottish that a genuine lady like myself tends to get lumped into the same category as flying haggis and bagpipes that survive on a diet of oatcakes and shortbread.

I even hear that many Americans actually believe that porridge is mined from pits sunk into the peat moors. Well even I know that this great breakfast dish comes from a plant. Wee men in kilts who dance jigs and shout 'Hoots mon!' as they load porridge slices onto surface bound trains are about as unlikely as me taking the kids for stroll over Culloden Moor on a wet Monday.

Then there's the haggis. What was it Rabbie Burns said again...
> Fair fa' your honest sonsie face,
> Great Chieftain o' the Puddin-race!
> Aboon them a' ye tak your place
> Painch, tripe or thairm:
> Weel are ye wordy of a grace
> As lang's my arm.

Most folk know these famous lines yet many of them still think that the haggis glides through the air and makes its nest in Highland forests.

*perhaps it is as well...*

*that balloon and bait*

*did NOT sail across...*

*the Loch as planned!*

Indeed, to listen to some folk, the haggis is an amazing fellow. Despite his clumsy appearance he can fly with the speed of a bullet and lay 20 eggs a day. The baby haggis can take to the air a few hours after being born and they learn to talk their language within a matter of days.

Haggis catchers, who are paid big money by butchers, risk a sharp bite on the jaws during chases and although a friendly creature when left alone, the haggis moves in for the kill if cornered.

With folk swallowing all this, if you'll pardon the expression, no wonder the non-believers who like to discredit me have it so easy.

One thing which I always find puzzling is the reputation which Scots have as meanies. We've all heard of the newspaper placard sign in Aberdeen, reputed to be the most tight-fisted city in Britain, which read: "Two local taxis collide: 34 persons injured." Then there is the picture of a flag day in Union Street... it's completely deserted. Of course the photographers who like to play that joke usually take their snaps at five in the morning.

I suppose it's true that my friends who live on land would like to have sporrans which laid fresh eggs for breakfast or whisky wells which brought liquid gold from the North Sea instead of black gold. But when it comes to having a good time and spending cash on worthwhile projects they're unbeatable.

What more proof do I need of this than all the chests full of silver and copper coins which the children have collected from the bed of the loch over the years.

They've been tossed in from boats and the shore by thousands of kind-hearted folk to wish me good luck. It's a pity I can't spend all this lovely lolly in the shops at Inverness or Fort Augustus.

*The American want folk to have picnics with me!*

# CHAPTER FOUR

STRANGE CREATURES known as water-kelpies lived here in ancient times.

They were half man and half horse with sharp teeth that could rip a human being into a thousand pieces according to John MacIntyre in *That's Scotland.* (Lang Syne: 90p).

He says: "Their powerful black hooves were strong enough to break every bone in a man's body and the neighing of kelpies was heard up to five miles away.

"They were violent beasts who used to lure travellers to a watery grave by pretending, at first sight, to be harmless.

"However, when a passer-by mounted his back the kelpie would shoot off at break neck speed to the loch...

"On one occasion a miser captured a kelpie and fitted it with a magic bridle. This effectively prevented the creature from returning to the loch.

"He made it work day and night dragging stones from a local quarry to a castle he was building.

"However, this source of slave labout was ended a few months later by one of the miser's enemies who freed the kelpie of the bridle.

"Without hesitating for a moment the beast bolted off to the loch cursing the miser as he went.

"Two days later a freak storm demolioshed the castle and the miser was killed by falling debris. During the following night all the stones vanished... and 48 hours after the storm had ended there was absolutely no trace of the castle."

*If any of you folks get a really clear picture of me then your fortune will be made.*

This is a story the children thoroughly enjoy and they always like me to to read it to them.

You may of course know that my dear sister, who never married, is still surviving and going strong over in Loch Morar. She is fine and good natured most of the time, but can become a wee bit hostile if humans get that bit too close for comfort. A few folk in boats have learned this and got quite a shock in the process.

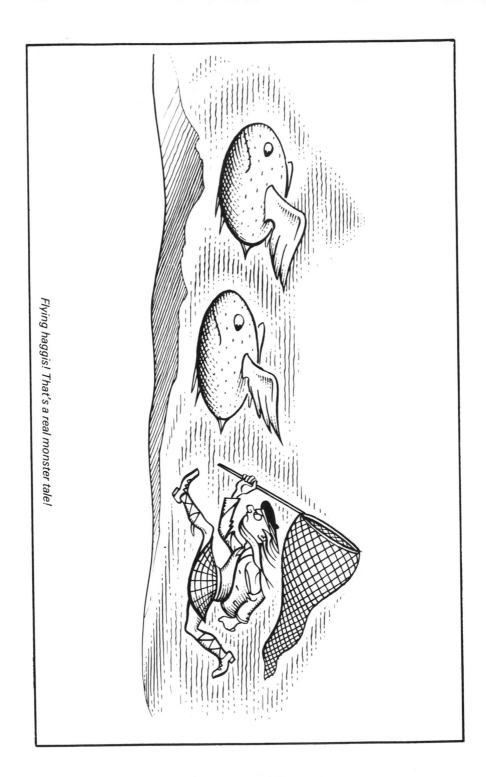

Flying haggis! That's a real monster tale!

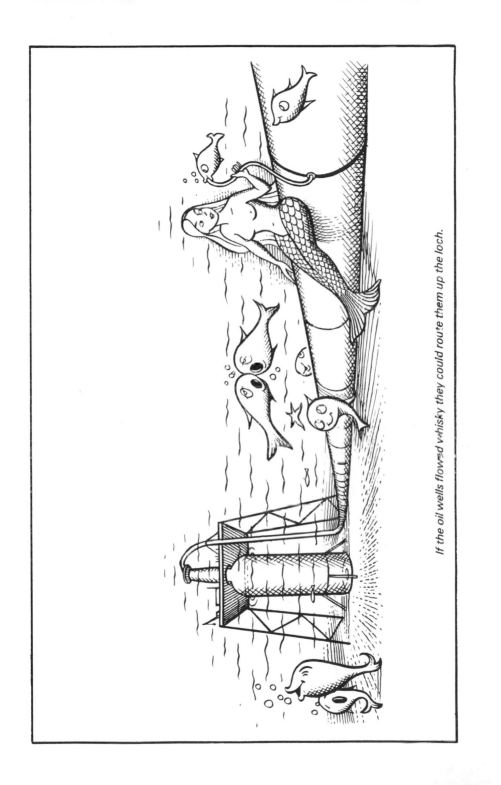

If the oil wells flowed whisky they could route them up the loch.

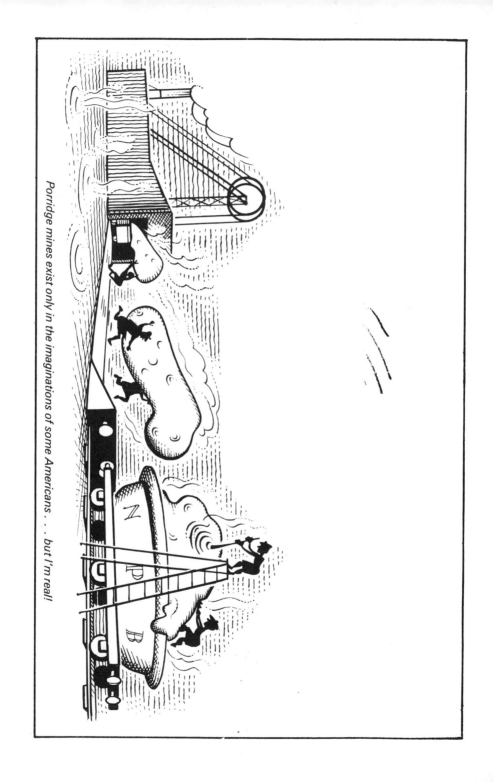

Porridge mines exist only in the imaginations of some Americans . . . but I'm real!

# CHAPTER FIVE

DID YOU KNOW...

THAT the surface area of the loch is 14,000 acres... it is 24 miles long and up to one and a half miles in width. Much of the loch is over 700 feet deep and in 1969 a mini-submarine went down as far as 820 feet and recorded 975 feet on its depth-sounding apparatus. The maximum depth of the loch is unknown

☆ ☆ ☆ ☆

THAT in 1933 the late Duke of Portland wrote to The Scotsman and The Times saying: "I should like to say that when I became, in 1895, the tenant of the salmon angling in Loch Oich and the River Garry, the forester, the hotelkeeper and the fishing ghillies used often to talk about a horrible great beastie as they called it, which appeared in Loch Ness."

☆ ☆ ☆ ☆

THAT the loch is believed to contain, prior to their spawning, 13 million adult salmon. Their total weight would be 65,000 tons and experts say that would provide a more than adequate food supply.

☆ ☆ ☆ ☆

THAT the water is peat-saturated and makes underwater photography very difficult because of reflection and scatter of light.

☆ ☆ ☆ ☆

THAT there have been some 10,000 reported sightings. It's estimated that about one third of these have been recorded in press stories, official reports and books.

☆ ☆ ☆ ☆

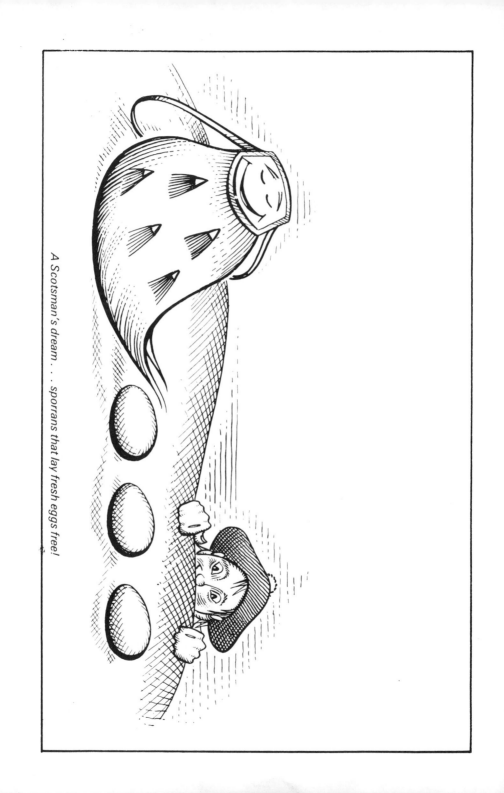

A Scotsman's dream . . . sporrans that lay fresh eggs free!

*THAT diver Duncan MacDonald refused to go into the loch again after a close encounter in 1880. His mission had been to inspect a sunken ship off the Fort Augustus entrance to the Caledonian Canal. Shortly after being lowered into the water he made urgent signals to be brought back up. The man was a complete nervous wreck and couldn't speak about his experience for several days. Eventually he told of seeing a large animal lying on the shelf of rock where the vessel was stuck firm. Said MacDonald: "It was a very odd looking beastie... like a huge frog."*

☆ ☆ ☆ ☆

THAT the loch never freezes. Its enormous depth and volume of water act as a kind of heater during the winter months. This effectively prevents snow from lying for long. The heat generated by the loch in winter is roughly equivalent to the energy given off by burning two million tons of coal.